What if you  a Home and you were naked and didn't know it?

Here's what they're saying nationally and it's no different where you are.

"Michael, SUPERB job taking me from a limited Auto, Home, and Umbrella policies where I thought I was adequately protected and just wasn't. It is so reassuring to have a specialist who protects me properly on my Autos & Home and even saved me thousands of dollars too! Way to go, Michael!"
>—Dave Langdon
>Toledo, OH

"The Carroll Insurance Group and Michael Carroll have impressed the daylights out of me by showing me where I had major gaps in protection that a specialist with Auto & Home Owners insurance picks up on right away. I would recommend that every Auto & Home Owner have Michael do a comparison where he does all of the work for you. It's a guaranteed win for you! You haven't met an insurance broker ever like Michael!"
>—Eric Bueter
>Wauseon, OH

"Michael Carroll does his job so well. It's great not to have to worry that something will go wrong because he knows everything and is so efficient. Even in non-crisis situations, his staff is helpful and tries to get me the best deal on coverage on my Auto & Home Owners. It's such a relief, under trying circumstances, to deal with people who know how to do their job and seem to have your best interests in mind."
>—Ed Dunaway
>Phoenix, AZ

THE NAKED INSURANCE AUTO & HOME OWNER

THE NAKED
INSURANCE
AUTO &
HOME OWNER

Leveraging the Multi-Billion Dollar
Auto & Home Insurance Industry
to Your Benefit

First edition 2013

ISBN: 978-1-62620-448-5

Cover art and all illustrations by Bruce Higdon (bhiggy28@gmail.com)

Acknowledgments

Writing a book for Auto & Home Owners—my favorite people outside of my own family—has always been a dream of mine, but one that seemed a long shot for a busy entrepreneur. Then, in the spring of 2011, while I was attending a seminar in Tampa, I had the good fortune to listen to Dr. Barry Lycka, an author and a publisher in his own right, who explained how doable writing and publishing a book could be if you had the right team and enough desire.

I won't say it wasn't a challenge, but I found that team, found that publisher, and now I hope you're going to be the beneficiary. My gratitude must go to the huge talent of illustrator Bruce Higdon. These people helped me bring all this work to its final form and made the whole process fun.

Finally—and this is a long way from formal politeness—I want to express my heartfelt gratitude to my wife of twenty-five years, Cheryl. She's my inspiration and my support and always will be.

And you, Auto & Home Owners, you're the basis of everything I do. Many thanks to you for taking the time to read what I have to say.

Table of Contents

Introduction

Greetings and thank you for taking time out of your busy schedule to read this book. I wrote *The Naked Insurance Auto & Home Owner* because I care about you and want to help you to prevent disasters that could potentially bankrupt you.

How I Came to Be an Auto & Home Owner Insurance Specialist

At the outset of my career, I worked for three years at Allstate where I won every award they had to offer. I had one of those Allstate "neighborhood offices" and always thought of myself as an independent agent. I wasn't, of course (I was an employee), but I still held onto that mindset.

As mentioned above at Allstate where I was an employee they have one set of guidelines and policies, so after three years I was ready to cut the umbilical cord and go out on my own. It was the best decision I ever made.

It was one of those serendipitous moments in life. I realized how much I really liked working with people who were hard working citizens who wanted what is best for their families. Most people shoot straight, give you their word and keep their word. They're warm and friendly, fun-loving and gregarious. It started me thinking: "These are the kind of people I want to do business with *all of the time*."

Once I made that decision, I placed myself under the tutelage of an old-time underwriter and loss-control professional who taught me every nook and cranny of exactly how to *properly* protect people's Autos, Homes, Boats, Motorcycles and RVs. Talk about tremendous mentoring—I received it!

Hard working people are also busy people. They have a demanding schedule with families to support and care for. They don't have time to micro-manage their insurance agent. They are looking for fewer headaches in their life, not more.

At the same time, it was clear to me that auto and homeowners are all different and to insure them all the same would be at best lazy and at worst incompetent. It was also clear to me that there were situations that could very quickly put people in the "poor house" if he or she was not insured correctly.

It was because of these possible dangers that I invested the time and effort to become schooled by my loss control/ underwriter mentor on every way an Auto and Homeowners should be insured. I committed myself at that point to give my future clients the very best that I could offer.

Reason for the Book

This little book is filled with examples of what can happen to an Auto and Home Owner who does not have adequate coverage. These are true stories with names and locations changed. This is a small sampling of the hundreds of horror stories that I have heard through my twenty-five plus years of working with Auto and Home Owners just like you.

I have found that most folks get their insurance coverage from an agent who would be considered a *generalist*. This type of agent is unaware of the particular needs specific to you. Oftentimes they don't know the difference between the needs of a family with numerous cars and drivers and a fancy house than a recent college graduate renting their first apartment. They tend to handle all folks in the same manner. Because they're generalists, their presentations lean toward "one size fits all."

A specialist is as important in the field of insurance as it is in the medical field. If you had a heart problem, you would want to be under the care of a heart specialist. Hopefully, it would be a cardiologist/heart surgeon with a proven reputation. A general practitioner would not do in such a case. Whether the medical problem was your own, or someone you cared about, you'd attempt to get the best care possible.

My Moral Decision

I'm not trying to see to it that every Auto and Home Owner is "insurance poor" but rather that each one is properly protected. Unlike life insurance agents, my commission is around 15%. So for those who are thinking all of this advice is being given out just to pad my pockets, the truth is that the add-ons discussed in this book make up a very small part of my income. However, each area holds the potential to ruin you. That's why I've made a moral decision to reveal the inside secrets of how you can leverage the vast resources of this multi-billion dollar industry for your financial well-being.

As you read through these chapters, ask yourself if this could happen to you. Do you know for sure if you're covered for any or all of these very possible disasters?

Stories like the ones in this book are heart-breakers for me, because I know that it didn't have to be that way. From property losses to massively underinsured liability limits: I've seen millions of dollars lost by unaware, uninformed—yes, *naked*—Auto and Homeowners. Some were actually put into bankruptcy.

None of these were my clients but many subsequently became my clients!

13

It Isn't Your Fault

1

Your

Fault

*Auto & Home Owners Have Been
Brainwashed About Choosing and Buying
Insurance Protection*

Stop and think. When you purchased your present Auto and Homeowners insurance coverage, was it from a buddy or a relative or a neighbor down the street? Or did you search the Internet or the Yellow Pages? Did you see a television commercial? If you own a business, perhaps it was one of your regular customers and you felt you wanted to return the favor. This last is certainly understandable in a business situation.

If any of the above fit your situation, don't think I intend to demean your decision-making procedures. However, for a moment let's compare this to a medical situation.

Similar to the Field of Medicine

As I asked earlier, would you have an eye, ears, nose and throat doctor operate on your knee? Or have a general practitioner perform open heart surgery? You don't just walk into any hospital and accept the first doctor you meet. If a loved one suffered from a disease that even the so-called specialists in your area were not qualified to treat, would you not then see about getting them to the Mayo Clinic, or a similar center of advanced medicine and treatments? If a case concerns someone you love, the decisions you make will be weighed heavily and you for sure will do your research and check out the doctor's background or history.

Inadvertently Putting You at Risk

Most Auto and Home Owners that I have come to know look at their home and even a favorite auto as a dearly-loved member of the family. For most, their home has actually *been* a part of the family for so many years. These are where the kids grew up, where eternal memories were made. In other words, this matters.....a bunch! In any case, your home for example is as important a venue as any in your life and you would never purposely put it in harm's way. Even at the most basic level, you probably have a security system in place and certainly lock all the doors at night.

Yet many Auto and Home Owners inadvertently put themselves in danger through simple negligence: they fail to select an insurance broker who is a seasoned specialist who properly insures Auto and Home Owners.

Obviously, there are insurance brokers in the property and casualty insurance field who have achieved a high degree of success. But the truth is that an insurance broker who is a generalist misses it almost every time when it comes to many of the dangers that I will relate in this book. Of course, they know to cover you for a fire, a slip and fall, or a tornado. Everyone knows that. But not every insurance broker understands about the hidden Auto and Home Owners-specific dangers that can put you out on the streets in a matter of days.

Chapter 1

IT ISN'T *YOUR* FAULT. AUTO & HOME OWNERS HAVE BEEN *BRAINWASHED.*

I'm going to demonstrate that you need a specialist who knows that area of expertise as well as they know anything, an insurance broker who specializes and for whom the Auto and Home Owners insurance industry is their number-one business.

Perhaps you've never even thought of your insurance in this way. If that's true, I fully understand. But that's the reason for this book. I want you informed and educated so you will never need to be at risk again. I'm here to bring you peace of mind and a better night's sleep.

Could This Happen to You?

Worse Yet, Would You Even Know?

Y ou know your auto and home are probably your greatest assets. But did you know they could also be a deadly liability? Did you know that it could cost you more money than you have right now?

This story may explain what I mean. Please read on.

Something's Wrong

T ony and Gina owned a beautiful home in a suburb of Columbus, OH. They built their dream house seven years ago.

As the family arrived back from a long day at their friend's cottage Tony parked the van in the driveway and walked toward their home. Opening the door was always a comfort to him. Truly *coming home.*

He stuck the key in the lock but it didn't feel right. *It was already unlocked.*

He pushed the door open and his heart sank. A quick scan of the premises told him this was going to be bad. Every room he entered was ransacked.

"Did they find the safe and Gina's jewelry box?" He ran to the study and to his desk. Sure enough, they had found the key to the safe.

How much cash had he left in the safe? His mind started to race. Who could do this sort of thing? Then he saw that his leather chair had been slashed! His heart started pounding with anger—or was it fear? He couldn't be sure.

If they'd slashed his chair that meant they'd done more than rip off money. They'd vandalized. He knew it wouldn't do much good, but it was time to call the cops.

As he sat there waiting for the police, his mind started to race. What other kinds of damage did they do? What else could go wrong? When was the last time he'd conducted a full inventory? Could these punks—or whoever did this—have damaged his computer too where all of the family's finances and school assignments were saved? What about their other vehicle? Was it still in the garage? Had he left spare keys in the study? Would all the locks have to be changed out?

Tony wandered back to the TV room. "Holy smokes!" he moaned. "Look at how much they took!"

What would he tell his family to calm them? How long would it take to get back to normal?

Would they have to wait almost a week before their home was livable? As the cold, hard facts began to settle in on him, Tony realized this could mean bad things crushing his finances.

The Panic Sets In

His thoughts then turned to his insurance agent. He'd never paid much attention to that policy. Always figured nothing would really go wrong. Now he really felt panicky. What was covered? What wasn't?

COULD *THIS* HAPPEN TO YOU? WORSE YET, WOULD YOU *EVEN KNOW?*

He began a mental survey of the people who work on the house. Could one of them have done this? "No, couldn't be. I've treated them like family."

He heard a knock on the door. The cops.

It took a few missed phone calls, but finally Tony caught up with his agent, Jim and relayed the whole sad story. The next day, Jim came down to Tony & Gina's home and walked through.

At the end of their tour Tony looked at Jim expectantly. "Well?" he said.

Tony could tell by the look on Jim's face there was something wrong.

Jim's eyes darted around the room. "Tony, I'm afraid we might have some problems."

What problems could Tony possibly have had? After all, all insurance policies cover theft, right?

True, theft *was* covered but it was the small print and the small details that were missing. Computers used in business weren't covered. Cash was limited as was jewelry. Various limitation in the policy meant that items besides cash that were actually stolen had limited or no coverage at all.

Unprepared Uninformed: Naked

As it turns out, Tony wasn't as prepared for this unfortunate event as he had thought. As a result, Jim was no longer Tony's insurance agent.

Tony was crushed.

Can you relate or do you know someone who can?

I'm here to say, *"It doesn't have to be this way!"*

You can have the dreams you cherish. You can count on the security you desire. You don't have to worry every day about something happening that's going to set you back.

What Can Go Wrong?

We know it's not just vandalism or theft. Heck, a lot goes wrong in anyone's neighborhood. It's the nature of owning a home.

Let's say a fire starts in the home next door. Your home suffers smoke damage. Who's responsible? Are you covered?

Let's take the scenario a bit further. Say this fire puts you out of your home for four months. At this point

- Who pays your rent while you live elsewhere and how much of it?
- Who pays your electricity, phone, water?
- Do you have enough cash flow to survive?
- Or will you lose your home—for something that was completely out of your control?

It doesn't seem fair, does it, but I've seen good people suffer needlessly because they didn't know the secrets of how to make the huge resources of the insurance industry work for them. I've been working with Auto and Homeowners for a long time and I've heard every horror story in the book.

If Tony had been my client, his problem would have been taken care of quickly and easily. Many times Home Owners like Tony have become my clients after they had a really serious claim. They wished they'd had me—an Auto and Homeowner insurance specialist—as their agent *before* the claim.

Tony Learns the Inside Secrets

A few weeks later Tony and I had just met. He was beaming. I knew this was the case when he said "Michael, you really told me the *inside secrets* of the insurance industry.

"I usually hate paperwork," he went on to say, "but I'm a businessman and I do have my life invested in my home. I now know more about protecting my Auto and Home for myself and my family than I ever thought was possible."

In one short meeting, I showed Tony:

- How to avoid the single biggest mistake Auto and Home Owners make in protecting themselves.
- The importance of having a broad market of insurance carriers to get the most complete coverage at the best price.
- The importance of having a risk analysis on your Auto and Homeowners insurance.

- The most powerful, proven seven-step system for protecting your Auto and Home for your future.

After his meeting with me, Tony felt more confident about his future. One meeting completely took away the cloud of uncertainty that had been hanging over his head for so long. Now he enjoyed peace of mind.

Are you reading this and wishing you also had access to this kind of information? Good news! That's exactly what *The Naked Insurance Auto & Home Owner* is all about.

3 The New Shiny Object:

Why to Avoid These Like the Plague

I f you watch any amount of television or are on the Internet I am sure you have been bombarded with auto insurer after auto insurer promising you savings all day every day.

From premium pricing guns to saving percentages equal to the time you spend deciding how to protect all of your assets, these new shiny objects have one intent and that is to grow their customer base with little regard on what is most important to you.

And what is most important to you is that when a claim happens.....and that is why you spend your hard-earned money protecting yourself with Auto & Home insurance...... that you are protected from catastrophic loss.

Yet, let's examine these "Shiny Objects" for what they really are which is nothing more than the absolute *wrong* way to purchase Auto & Homeowners insurance.

Gimmicks Galore

Specifically, having a gimmick where you input a price that you want to pay for your Auto & Homeowners insurance is as foolish a concept as drinking poison and here is why. This mentality does not take into account what you have and what you earn that dictate how much protection you must always buy on your Auto & Homeowners insurance.

See the pricing difference comes between different insurers that a true professional Independent Insurance Broker who specializes in Auto & Homeowners insurance will get for you with absolutely the correct limits of protection you need and at the correct best pricing. Period. No quick fixes or gimmicks.

The Generalists Versus the Specialist

In fact a generalist when you get a comparative quote will copy what you have now taking no regard for what you need to protect you and your family from financial ruin. The term "comparing apples to apples" is too often that game of "dumb and dumber" at its absolute best.

And calling an 800 number or buying over the Internet is truly a game of Russian Roulette which almost always ends up in your financial death as who assists you there? No one or a customer service rep is who. Is that who you really want advising or assisting you and much more often than not at higher premiums to boot?

Also, let's examine taking an amount of time that will equate into savings on your Auto & Homeowners insurance. Say for example you spend 16 minutes on getting a comparative quote, does that means you get 16% savings?

You get my point by now, I'm hoping, on how silly these concepts can be.

Chapter 3

THE *NEW SHINY OBJECT:* WHY TO *AVOID* THESE LIKE THE *PLAGUE!*

So as you can see the "New Shiny Object" is really nothing more than aggressive marketing aimed at customer acquisition with little to no regard to what is best for you which will absolutely ultimately ruin you.

Yet the great news, as you'll discover in the following chapters is that you will be able to turn the tables on the insurance industry and be able to get the correct amount of protection you need on your Auto & Homeowners insurance at the very best pricing!

How to
Properly
Protect
Yourself
with the
Correct
Liability
Limits
on Your
Auto Insurance

As shared in the previous chapter being distracted with the latest "Shiny Object" is no way to buy your Auto & Homeowners insurance.

So enough of what not to do and what to avoid. Here is where I am going to share a massive insurance insider secret where you can absolutely protect what is most likely your biggest liability exposure all day every day. And that is your autos where you and everyone in your family is one accident away from turning your financial world upside down.

By that I mean none of us ever intends to get into an accident as the vast majority of us really try hard to abide by all driving laws. Yet even with that being said, accidents still happen due to poor driving conditions, faulty cars, or just plain human error. It happens and is why you pay your hard earned money on Auto insurance.

So here is how you decide what liability limits you must carry. The litmus test is twofold:

1) Take the approximate value of your home and that is the "each person" liability limit that you must carry to protect you properly

2) Take your annual income plus savings, retirement accounts, and investment portfolio and add that as to what limit of liability limit you must carry

Let's examine both points above and how it applies in what I see all day every day.

Dave and Julie have the model family. Three kids, an incredibly nice home, and some nice vehicles.

This Is Where It Matters

Dave and Julie's home is worth $275,000. They have four cars as their oldest two are driving. Dave is a business man and makes approximately $150,000 annually. Julie is a stay at home mom after the kids were born. Prior to having kids she amassed a retirement account from her career that is now worth $200,000.

Like most folks Dave had a friendly neighborhood insurance agent who had written his and Julie's insurance when they were first married 21 years ago. At that time both Julie and Dave were fresh out of college and renting a house so the common liability limits of $100,000 each person and $300,000 each accident along with property damage of $100,000 seemed about right.

Yet as time went on their agent retired. Around that same time they built their dream home and decided to get a quote from another well-known hands on insurer who did an "apples to apples" comparison because it is all about price, right? WRONG!

Dave and Julie never thought much about their Auto insurance as they drive safely and what claims they'd have would be

HOW TO *PROPERLY* PROTECT YOURSELF WITH THE *CORRECT LIABILITY LIMITS* ON YOUR AUTO INSURANCE.

of the minor variety. Glass claims from stones to the windshield, a road disablement twice, and a parking lot fender bender.

Never when their Son and Daughter were added to the policy was it ever mentioned by their so called insurance professional agent to raise their liability limits. And the mentality here is the current agent is afraid they will lose the policy at a time when adding a young driver adds premium already and they are afraid they "shop" them. How pathetic and so wrong yet it happens the vast majority of the time.

"The Accident"

Dave was driving home from his office one evening as a nasty snow storm ensued. Dave was always a cautious driver as was the case that evening. Yet conditions were so bad that Dave's vehicle began to slide and ultimately he lost control causing a pretty nasty wreck where Dave was at fault.

Dave was banged up pretty good with bumps and bruises and a few cuts yet thankfully nothing major. The vehicle Dave hit was heavily damaged and the two occupants hurt where an ambulance had to take them to the hospital with undisclosed injuries.

Dave called his insurance agent who promptly returned his call the next morning at 9:30 a.m. (yes that is sarcasm and will be address in a forthcoming chapter). Dave was instructed how to get a rental car and how his car would be repaired less his deductible. Dave asked about the folks to whom he ran into and his agent had no information.

It All Comes Apart

In about two weeks Dave and his vehicle are like brand new which leaves him very pleased. Still in the back of his mind Dave feels badly for the other vehicles occupants and wishes he knew how to say he was sorry yet figures that is why he has insurance as they will make them whole.

And if Dave's liability limits were sufficient that would indeed be the case yet as shared earlier in this chapter Dave and Julie carry limits of $100,000 each person and $300,000 each accident for personal injury liability. Which again means *only* $100,000 each person is available and not $300,000.

About six months later Dave receives a frantic call from Julie sharing that in that day's mail they were served with a lawsuit for Dave's accident. Dave calms Julie and shares to scan and email it to the claims adjuster as they will take care of it.

Roughly two weeks later Dave gets a call from the adjuster Bob who says to him, "Dave I think you may have a problem and wanted to alert you to a reservation of rights letter and what that means for you that I am sending to your house today."

In a nutshell what Bob the claims adjuster told Dave was that he does not have enough liability limits to cover what the injured parties Lawyer is demanding via a lawsuit.

Dave replies to Bob, "Well Bob this is just a ruse shooting high and they settle for less, right?"

Bob's reply, "Dave it would be in your best interest to hire a Lawyer." Dave felt physically ill upon hearing this.

A Specialist Knows How To Protect You Properly Every Time

The Auto & Homeowner insurance specialist knows and understands about how to determine the correct liability limits, and not only is aware of how much liability you must carry, but also knows exactly which insurance companies offer the best pricing and claims representation.

Back to our medical comparisons. There may be hundreds of heart surgeons around the country, but the top surgeons work out of about five primary hospitals. These centers are known for their premier heart surgeons.

In the same way, as a specialist, I'm acquainted with each of the top insurance companies and the specialties that each one offers.

The surprise for most Auto and Home Owners is that this kind of coverage is extremely affordable. The problem is not that such coverage is cost prohibitive. The problem is lack of knowledge and lack of awareness.

If you find you do not sufficient liability limits, you are well within your rights to fire your generalist agent right now! Your financial livelihood is at stake, after all.

Now What?

Well Dave and Julie sat down with their Lawyer and the Lawyer of their insurance company and the news was grim. The driver sustained injuries that would limit his ability to physically enjoy activities that came naturally to him as he was quite active.

Surgeries, rehab, and ultimately damages would get well into *the hundreds of thousands of dollars.* Julie started to get teary eyed.

Because they only carried liability limits of $100,000 each person that means that the rest would come via a lien attached to Dave and Julie's home and seizing of any available investment accounts.

Dave and Julie's insurance company paid the $100,000 and walked away as that was their full obligation.

And Dave and Julie's Lawyer was able to work a fair deal that they would "only" have to pay $400,000 where more like double that would have been a slam dunk case. In effect though Dave and Julie were back to square one financially speaking where they had to surrender all assets and sell their dream home to pay off the injured party.

It Doesn't Have to Be This Way Ever

The absolute shame of Dave and Julie's story is when they were referred to me is that it didn't have to be that way ever yet is by far the rule than the exception in that the vast majority of insurance agents along with 800 numbers and online insurers have not a clue as to how to properly protect you again adhering to a "one size fits all mentality."

When I sat down with Dave and Julie and heard their plight the shame of it all is that had they been advised properly and carried $500,000 each person on their liability limits and a $1,000,000 Excess Liability policy none of this would have happened.

And many reading this may say, "well that must cost huge money to do all of that and I cannot afford that!" When the reality is two-fold in that you cannot afford *not* to do this even if finances are indeed that tight. Plus in real dollars to increase to these limits may cost all of around $30 per month. Read that again around $30 per month!

There is a comeback feel-good part to the story of Dave and Julie. Since the kids were getting older Julie wanted to resume her career, and Dave earned an ownership position in his company which doubled his income which allowed them to buy a new home to their liking.

5 Young Drivers It's Time2Drive®

For any of us that have children driving or will, this chapter will resonate with you at some level. The intent of this chapter is to keep up to speed with the risks that young drivers face today that weren't there years ago.

If you were anything like my wife and I were when our oldest backed out of the driveway for the first time, we said The Rosary over and over again.

All kidding aside, we all have witnessed first-hand or have seen on TV or in the newspaper the severity of auto accidents and worry about the inexperienced young driver, especially our own children.

And for today's young drivers they are faced with risks that were nonexistent when we were kids most notably cell phones where distracted driving via talking or texting is proven to be as bad as driving drunk. Factor in that over 90% of all Americans have a cellular device and that is a massive risk to say the least.

Factor in that drivers under the age of 21 prefer texting or typing on a social media platform over talking on the phone which is the most dangerous form of distraction as it takes your eyes completely off of the road and this is a major issue for which to address!

In fact, as you'll read in the rest of this chapter everyone pays this subject lip service yet only those who truly care about making a difference do as my firm does.

Time2Drive®

Time2Drive® is an interactive, teen-driving program focused on the common risks young drivers face. The program teaches teens and their parents how to be safer on the road and stresses the dangers of driving intoxicated and driving distracted.

A Fun, Interactive Experience

Time2Drive® is designed to be hands-on. Teens will get to try on Fatal Vision Goggles® that reinforce the dangers of impaired driving. Plus, they'll have the chance to get behind the wheel of a driving simulator that shows just how scary driving distracted can be. Both the goggles and the simulator share a powerful message of which the young driver will benefit.

What Types of Activities Make Up the Program?

The program is structured around audience participation with group discussions and activities designed to enhance the learning experience. Because more than half of teen accidents are alcohol or drug related—part of the program is devoted to the dangers of impaired driving. Teens can participate in several demonstrations and hands on activities. The program ends with parents and their young drivers working together to create a Parent/Teen Driving

Chapter 5

YOUNG DRIVERS, IT'S TIME2DRIVE®

Commitment that defines restrictions, privileges, rules and consequences.

Additional Benefits for You and Your Young Driver

♦ Time2Drive® is an opportunity to help teens become safe drivers, make your community a safer place and help reduce the possibility of future tragedies

♦ Time2Drive® encourages teens and adults to think about the consequences of poor decisions made on the road

- Motor vehicle crashes are the number one killer of teens.
- Time2Drive® brings the community closer together.
- Community members can become better educated about their state's teen driving laws.
- Attendees will be actively involved in activities and demonstrations.
- Time2Drive® is FREE for the community.

The Time2Drive® commitment is a proven difference maker for all young drivers and am hoping your teen driver can experience this!

Two last comments that often get missed for young drivers driving up their premiums. The first is if your child carries a "B" or better average in school they qualify for what is normally a 20% discount which is huge.

The second comment is once your child goes off to school over 100 miles away without a vehicle they get the "adult rate" from there on out until they graduate or take a car down to school with them. Again a massive discount and make certain that you get the premium reduction if this applies to you.

Pizza
Delivery

I'll keep this chapter short and sweet. Repeat after me. My auto insurer most likely will not cover me or any driver in my household or owned vehicle for Pizza Delivery.

Pizza is here to stay. A winner for families on the go. Tasty, cheap, and filling! And with this industry continuing to grow many of you reading this book either are, have, want to, or at least know someone who delivers pizza.

And you know what? Easily 90% of all personal auto insurers specifically *exclude* pizza delivery for any type of claim.

Therefore, if you or a family member must deliver pizza to make ends meet, by all means request a copy of your employers insurance coverage limits for Pizza Delivery (should be at least $1,000,000) and if your exposure discussed in Chapter 3 is less than $1,000,000 than you are fine yet if it is not then you or your household driver should not deliver pizzas ever!

PIZZA DELIVERY.

Auto Insurance Deductibles and Worthy "Bells & Whistles"

This is where folks miss out too often and it comes back to haunt them as I'll address in this chapter. Don't get misled that these are the same as maintenance warranties on an appliance as these are the most common claims that you'll experience and will make hundreds if not thousands of dollars a year difference whether in covered claims or premiums.

This chapter will not be so much in a story example format yet in a definition type format as it reads much better for you that way too.

Deductibles

This subject of deductibles on your Auto insurance gets discussed on a regular basis as most folks are relatively astute in this arena. Yet before assuming everyone is in on this subject, let's address physical damage coverage on your Auto insurance.

What Is Collision Coverage?

Collision coverage protects your vehicle if you are at fault in an accident or if you are either hit and run or hit by an uninsured motorist. Those last two examples I specifically include as folks decide to drop their Collision deductible on an older yet still somewhat valuable vehicle to save maybe $150 annually may not be the best idea. The litmus test is easy here. Since you should always carry at the least a $500 Collision deductible and what that premium costs to carry that and estimate how many more years you wish to drive your vehicle is when to decide to drop Collision coverage or keep it.

For example if you had a 10 year old vehicle that was worth $5,000 with a $500 deductible where the Collision premium is $150 annually. You also hope to drive it five more years and taking into consideration the vehicle will drop say 10% every year so $500 in value annually which means in five years it will be worth $2,500.

Add the lowest value to today's value which would be $7,500 and divide it in half which would be $3,750 in this example. Then subtract five years of $150 in premium which would be $750 which leaves you at $3,000 less the $500 deductible which would be $2,500.

So if $2,500 is chump change to you or a loss you can afford then by all means drop your Collision deductible.

What Is Comprehensive Coverage?

Comprehensive coverage for your vehicle is everything that can happen to the physical damage of your vehicle other than a Collision. Common examples, would be fire, theft, vandalism, and glass breakage.

A not so commonly known claim that is covered under comprehensive coverage is running into an animal (usually a

AUTO INSURANCE *DEDUCTIBLES* PLUS WORTHY *"BELLS & WHISTLES."*

deer). Comprehensive coverage claims do not count against your premiums being raised as they are normally not your fault.

Simply put in today's day and age no one should carry less than $500 deductibles on their collision or comprehensive coverage. The premiums are geared for best savings starting at those deductible levels.

Valuable Bells & Whistles on Your Auto Insurance

There are many "dirt cheap" cost wise add-ons that you'll find to be worth hundreds if not thousands of dollars. The following are what most insurers offer and certainly the best insurers offer always:

Safety Glass Coverage

This incredibly valuable coverage offers you a zero deductible for any glass claim which is by far the most common claim for Auto insurance. Also, this does not impact your premium as it is rarely your fault. Insurers that offer this first class protection also have a direct relationship with a glass repair or replacement company where they come right out to where ever you are at the time of loss if need be.

Rental Reimbursement

You must carry physical damage on the vehicle to carry this valuable protection. This affords you a rental car coverage if your vehicle is damaged and in a repair shop. Without it you best hitch a ride or get out your walking shoes.

First Accident & First Ticket Forgiveness

Usually well worth the nominal premiums to avoid any surcharges if you are at fault in an auto accident or pick up a moving violation.

Roadside Assistance

This is an excellent benefit for you and your family and between $20–$40 annually total as it protects not only all of your vehicles for any type of roadside assistance plus also all household members while even a passenger in a vehicle too!

From a flat tire, to a dead battery, or to locking your keys in your car this coverage would apply and again even if you are a passenger in a friend's vehicle this can apply too!

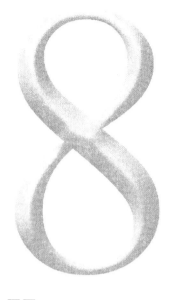

How to Properly Protect Yourself with the Correct Coverage on Your Home Insurance

Whether you own a home, a condo, or rent where you live is where your life is. It is where you eat, sleep, relax, and spend time with people of your choice be it family or friends.

So protecting what you own where you live is as serious and important as it gets. I cannot share how many times I have heard renters share that they don't need any protection for their belongings and when disaster strikes they are completely ruined. And to save literally $200 a YEAR!

And for those of us who own a home or a condo we would not sleep a wink knowing that our greatest investment is at risk, wouldn't we? Yet hold on tight because what you are about to discover is going to rock your world as the horror stories I have seen over the last 25 plus years are beyond comprehension as it did not have to be that way.

This chapter much as the Auto insurance chapter too will be a listing of what you can and should carry to best protect you as a great reference point.

Water

Good old water. Has all kinds of benefits in life. Yet for a homeowner it can be a huge monster as I'll share. Water is the number cause of loss on Homeowners insurance. The following list will share what is and what isn't protected on a "regular" homeowner's policy:

1) *Rain leaks in from your roof.* The initial rain leaking in and causing damage is covered yet you have to immediately stop the damage. If your roof was old and needed replacement, that is not covered as wear and tear and is always excluded.

2) *Heavy rains caused sewers to back up and your basement or downstairs takes on water.* This is excluded unless you have a special endorsement for "Sewer Back-up" which the lowest limit you should select is $10,000 which on average costs around $75 annually.

3) *Heavy rains cause a flood where outside waters penetrate your home.* Excluded always unless you have a separate Flood Insurance policy where there is a 60 day minimum waiting period.

4) *Pipes burst causing water damage.* Covered unless the home was vacant for more than 30 days.

5) *A toilet or bathtub or washer or dishwasher overflows.* Covered.

All of these are subject to your Homeowners insurance deductible and are of course subject to specific policy provisions yet as a rule of thumb the above will be very accurate.

Jewelry & Other Valuable Items

All insurers exclude Jewelry for damage and mysterious disappearance unless you schedule each piece which also eliminates your deductible. The average cost to schedule jewelry is about $9 per

HOW TO *PROPERLY PROTECT* YOURSELF WITH THE *CORRECT COVERAGE* ON YOUR HOME INSURANCE.

thousand annually. Any piece over $5,000 normally requires an appraisal.

Other valuable items such as furs, silverware, card and stamp collections, and fine arts have limited coverage and should be scheduled too for frankly nominal insurance costs.

Other Cool Bells & Whistles

There are a myriad of other "dirt-cheap" cost yet valuable protection for you to buy such as:
1) Equipment Breakdown which acts as a maintenance policy to repair or replace any mechanical in your home due to sudden and accidental breakdown. Items such as your electronics from your TVs to your computers to HVAC systems fall under this approximately $30 annual endorsement.
2) Earthquake. Plain and simple if you live in a risk area absolutely get this must protection yet even if you live in a non-earthquake area it may be worth the cost just in case.
3) Identity Theft. A no brainer and runs usually around $45 annually to repair your identity in full.

Liability & Medical Payments

Often forgotten about until something "odd" happens. By odd for Liability protection what would happen if your dog bit someone? Or if one of your kids punched out another kid at a party or ballgame? Or if you hit a golf ball into someone's windshield or picture window? Or someone slips and falls on your property?

These all fall under your Liability section of your Homeowners insurance policy and aren't as uncommon as you may have thought prior.

Medical Payments fall into the category where someone injures themself on your property yet you are definitively not negligent. Examples of this are someone spraining an ankle playing backyard hoops, or by missing a step. The "Klutz Clause" as I like to call this great coverage as it will help your guest defer costs with health insurance co-pays and deductibles.

Discounts Anyone?

For a new home or a recently renovated home there are big discounts available. Plus if you have an alarm system, the more elaborate the bigger the discount. Plus all insurance companies will start discounting on one end and surcharging on the other for properly maintained or not maintained roofs as hail damage has become a billion dollar loser on already average and below roofs.

Condo & Renters

Both Condos and Renters have unique risks inherent only to them. For Condo owners Loss Assessment is a huge and very inexpensive add on that is a must and at a limit of $50,000 to protect you from getting an insurance related assessment from your Condo Association.

Also, Condo owners must always have the correct amount of building coverage as this is by far the most poorly written part of any Condo policy. 90% plus have grotesquely under-insured coverage here. Make certain this is not you!

And Renters always select Replacement Cost on your contents. It isn't worth the approximately $50 annual savings to get depreciated value for all of your belongings.

9

People Just Like You

Your Best Friends

To get the best insurance coverage that is specific to you as an Auto & Home Owner, a key strategy is to retain an agent who specializes in Auto & Homeowner insurance.

You don't want an insurance company employee for your agent. You want someone who's going to work for *you*, not someone whose paycheck is tied to one company. You need an agent who can shop the market, compare prices, and get the most comprehensive coverage for you—maybe even use multiple companies for your total coverage.

You want a good price? And you want ultimate protection when disaster strikes? Use an independent agent who specializes in Auto & Homeowner insurance.

There's a lot of money involved in buying insurance and you want to make sure it works for you. Don't trust the financial protection of everything you own to an insurance agent who is not a specialist with Auto and Home Owners and the special problems you face every day!

Huge Industry

Insurance is a huge industry. There's insurance for everything. Anything you can have, do, own, or manage, there's insurance for it. And no one agent can specialize in all of it. In fact, a professional independent agent can only specialize in a few niches and really understand them.

Insurance is a very technical business. Policies, coverage, endorsements, exclusions—it has a language all its own. Also, the insurance needs of each industry are highly specific. Just because someone specializes in insuring huge manufacturing concerns, doesn't mean they know anything about the special needs of Auto and Home Owners. And just because your wife's cousin sells insurance, doesn't mean he's the guy with whom you want to trust your financial health!

Let's look at a few other things that you are *not* looking for:

♦ An agent or an agency that tries to sell you their services on meaningless platitudes like "quality" or "excellence." Those are just buzzwords that mean very little.

♦ An agency that tries to sell you on their services because they've "been around since 1934" or some such nonsense. Yes, you want a professional that has thoroughly studied the business, but what do you care what they were doing in 1934? Believe me, insurance back then wasn't anything like it is today.

♦ An agent who doesn't know Auto and Home Owners. I've said it before and I'll say it again: You wouldn't want a foot doctor to perform surgery on your heart, would you? I didn't think so. So don't trust your financial well-being to just any insurance agent.

Over the long haul, you will be in a much better position when your agent is not only an Auto & Homeowner insurance specialist, but also is recognized and awarded for their commitment to your well-being!

Chapter 9

PEOPLE JUST LIKE *YOU:* YOUR *BEST FRIENDS!*

Lead by Example

Additionally, I lead by example. The strategies that I shared in this book I have used for 25 plus years with my clients, family, and friends and absolutely for myself!

I don't think in terms of nine-to-five, as my phones are answered by a live person 24/7. I think in terms of how you work and operate. Claims don't happen within regular business hours only and I'm available to my clients whenever.

I'm there for my current clients; I will be there for you as well!

Some Final Words

There you have it. I've asked you to follow me on a journey through the unthinkable and the unimaginable. But these things happened to real people—people who made their livings just the way you do. I've brought things to your attention you may have never before considered, things you maybe don't really want to think about, but they're real and they're out there. I want to see you get to the place where you never have to worry about, or be concerned about such matters. That confidence will free you up to do what you do best—enjoy your life with no insurance worries ever!

Thank you for investing your time to learn more about how an Auto & Homeowner insurance specialist works and how it can benefit you. I know your time is valuable, so I trust this was a helpful experience that will change forever how you look at possible disasters and catastrophes.

There was no mention of Motorcycle insurance, RV insurance, Boat insurance, Rental Property insurance, or Umbrella insurance (highly recommend all homeowners get an additional $1,000,000 Umbrella Liability policy) yet this can be discussed if you own these "toys."

Lastly, take literally all of 5 minutes to get a comparison done on your Auto & Homeowners insurance to stop from being "insurance naked," simply email (michael@cigvip.com) or send to my private fax (1-866-908-2508) your current coverage pages and handwrite in all drivers' names, dates of birth, and driver's license numbers.

Receipt of the information will be confirmed immediately. Within 48 hours a first class super reader friendly analysis will be sent to you. All the comparisons will be done for you too. Yes, it is really that easy!

So what are you waiting for? Act today, right now while you are thinking of this as I *guarantee* you this to be time well spent!

Michael Carroll
419-897-0101
michael@cigvip.com

About the Author

Michael Carroll was born in Bangor, Maine. His family moved to Toledo, Ohio, when he was a small child and there he still resides with his bride of over twenty years, Cheryl (Sisinyak) Carroll, and three children, Catie, Patrick, and Joey.

Michael has spent the last twenty-five years helping to protect Auto & Homeowners. He is considered a specialist in his field of insurance and one can quickly sense his passion for the service he provides and the message he has to share with Auto and Home Owners all around the country.

In September, 2012, and for the 12th consecutive year, The Carroll Insurance Group, LLC was selected as a *Best Practices Agency*. This insurance company qualified for this status by ranking among the top performers in the annual Best Practices Study conducted by the Independent Insurance Agents & Brokers of America (IIABA) and Reagan Consulting. They were awarded Best Practices top 195 out of 37,500 independent agencies nationally.

More than 800 out of 37,500 insurance firms from around the country were nominated in six revenue categories ranging from "Under $1.25 Million" in annual revenue to "Over $25 Million" in annual revenues. More than 300 agencies submitted data. Only 195 agencies scored high enough to qualify for inclusion. (Just for reference, this is the equivalent of being in the top five college football program year in and year out. Or like being a perennial Super Bowl contender.)

Carroll Insurance Group has offices in Maumee, Ohio, which is a suburb of Toledo, and in Phoenix, Arizona. Having both offices allows Michael to travel (which he loves to do) all over the country to ultimately meet many of his favorite people—Auto & Homeowners just like you!